HELD

*A mother's journey of praying
for a prodigal*

Torn Curtain Publishing
Wellington, New Zealand
www.torncurtainpublishing.com

ISBN Softcover 978-0-6453977-1-0

Cover design by Noelle Savill

Cataloguing in Publishing Data
    Title: Held
    Author: Eleanor Formaggio
    Subjects: Christian living, parenting teens, spiritual growth, prayer

A copy of this title is held at the National Library of Australia.

- Journalling Guide Included -

HELD

*A mother's journey of praying
for a prodigal*

Eleanor Formaggio

FOREWORD

WHAT YOU HAVE BEFORE YOU IS A book that contains rich wisdom from the trenches of a mother's journey of not only contending for her son's faith, but also one of discovering the passion of her heavenly Father for her own soul. Whilst none of us in our right minds would pray for trials or spiritual battles, nevertheless we see that God uses these seasons to do a work inside of us that may never have occurred had we not encountered them. This is a book about tragedy, loss, fear, and disappointment as well as hope, faith, love, prayer and perseverance. I highly endorse not just the book and the wisdom it contains, but also the author. Eleanor is a passionate lover of God, her husband, and her children. She is a prayer warrior, and a woman of God who has a calling to inspire and raise up men and women of God to know how to raise great families and partner with Him in every season of that journey.

David Balestri
Kingdom Life Coach
Sydney, Australia

CONTENTS

INTRODUCTION

NONE OF US EXPECT OUR CHILDREN TO go off the rails or to abandon the values and beliefs we have raised them with. And yet, as we discovered firsthand, it's a common experience—especially during the teenage years.

For us, life had been going along smoothly. We felt like we'd done a fairly good job of the early years with our kids. We were secure in our parenting and enjoyed a close sense of belonging and togetherness in our family. Then, as our firstborn entered high school, we began to sense a gradual shift in his attitudes. Like storm clouds rolling in from a distance on an otherwise clear sunny day, we hoped it would all come to nothing, that any teenage angst would be short-lived and quickly blow over. Instead, we found ourselves in the midst of one of the greatest battles of our lives.

This book is not so much our son Daniel's story, as my own—the story of a mum whose child slowly slipped into a lifestyle we would never have imagined. As Christians we always expected the best for our children. We believed God had given them to us, entrusting them to our care, but ultimately, we trusted Him for our children's future and wellbeing. Parenting a prodigal tested the depths of that trust. But it also proved it.

What I discovered was that God was not only looking out for Daniel even when he wandered far—He was taking me on a journey as well. There were many struggles that came with parenting a child who wasn't walking in the ways I had endeavoured to raise him in.

This was an intensely personal journey, both painful and spiritually enlightening. All throughout, God was revealing to me more about Himself. It was a season of learning, leaning in and listening. It was also a time of longing and loving, not only for me, his mum, but also for those who loved our boy as we did—his siblings, friends, and extended family.

Going into this challenging season of life, I already knew the power of unconditional love and acceptance. Now, as the mother of a prodigal, I had to learn to contend for the lives of those we love the most. I have discovered what God can do when we take our hands off a situation, not in resignation, but in complete trust in the only One who saves: Jesus. My son's prodigal story has given me a story of my own!

Most Christians are aware of the parable of the prodigal son. It's a story Jesus told in which a son decides to ask his father for his inheritance prematurely. He wants to leave, to live his own life and make his own way, to be free. Rebelling against any sense of responsibility or obligation, he leaves the comfort and peace of his father's house. But after some time, maybe years later, when he has hit rock bottom, he comes to his senses, realises he needs his father, and returns home (Luke 15:11-19).

Waiting for our prodigals to come home is a terrible experience. Every day can feel like ten years. But we must trust that God knows the right time to pull them out of the mire, and believe me, He's careful not to do it a moment too soon! We often prefer to try pulling them out of their situation ourselves, but the outcome (or 'fruit') will never be the same as if God does the rescuing in His time and His way. Luke 7:47 tells us that those who have been forgiven much love much. When our children have personally experienced the lengths the Father will go to rescue and restore them, they will not easily be snatched from Jesus' hands again (John 10:28).

In the waiting, however, we must be careful that our trust does not become passive. Instead, we are called to partner with God. One

2

of the primary ways we do this is through prayer. But often we pray from a human perspective, when what we really need is to pray with insight into God's heart and mind for our child. We can end up praying generally, when what we need is a vision. We need a vision of the person our child was created to be, and then we need to continually remind ourselves (and them!) of who they truly are, because it's not just us who are losing our children; they've lost themselves. There's a veil over their eyes that our words and prayers can help to remove.

The saying, 'The greater the call, the greater the battle' is especially true during our children's formational teenage years. That's why it's so important that we determine we will not partner with fear, terror, despair, hopelessness, guilt, self-condemnation, frustration, blame, or even a compromised version of what God had in mind. God knows who our children are destined to be. For almost two years my son chose the pig pen over the Father's house. Throughout those years it felt as if God's plans for his life were in disarray. I now understand, however, that Daniel has a strong evangelistic gift on his life—and that he needed to go through this journey to have a revelation of what it is to move from darkness to light.

Sadly, the topic of prodigal children is often taboo. We soon found that people would rather not ask how Daniel was than hear the truth. This wasn't anyone's fault. It's not easy to wade into someone else's situation. The reality is, we were ashamed to speak about it too. There's a sense of failure that accompanies parenting a prodigal child and a fear of being judged. But we need to have these conversations because not only does God have hope for your child, He has hope for you as a parent.

In these pages I've recorded for you my personal experiences and internal battles, memories of conversations between my husband and myself, my conversations with our son, as well as my crying out to God during that time. There is something about painful memories. Those moments that carried such a weight of emotion are etched like carvings in wood in my mind. I have done my best to recreate them for you with as much of the detail as I can remember so that I can walk alongside you in your own journey. My hope in sharing our story is that it will provide you with strategies to empower you to fight for the future of your child and to partner with God for the destiny on their life. God gave me some wonderful prophetic images that sustained me and helped me to pray with focus. As I describe those images and share the lessons I learned from them, I pray that you may also have renewed hope and faith for your child to return to relationship with the living King and become a child of God.

Jesus came to save all, even when they are in the darkest place we could imagine. I want to remind you of this: He is able to call those who are lost. But you are not just a spectator to this miracle. You have a pivotal part to play in the restoration of your child. You get to partner with God for the outcome He has purposed. And while that partnering is often painful, it is also a privilege. Good is going to come from your story—even if the journey is longer than you would like. And in the end, it's not only your child who will have a story of redemption. You will too as you lean into God and learn to partner with Him.

I can no longer recognise what my spiritual life was like before these events; it is so much deeper, so much *richer*. God wants you to have the same testimony. He wants to lead not only your child, but also you as a parent—as *His child*—to a place of restoration with one another and with Him. He wants intimacy, wholeness, and strength for you *both*.

THE LEAVING

- Wandering from Home -

Jesus continued: "There was a man who had two sons. The younger one said to his father, 'Father, give me my share of the estate.' So he divided his property between them.

Not long after that, the younger son got together all he had, set off for a distant country and there squandered his wealth in wild living. After he had spent everything, there was a severe famine in that whole country, and he began to be in need. So he went and hired himself out to a citizen of that country, who sent him to his fields to feed pigs. He longed to fill his stomach with the pods that the pigs were eating, but no one gave him anything."

Luke 15:11-16

1

COPING WITH DISENGAGEMENT

I REMEMBER WHEN MY SON DANIEL WAS YOUNGER. Forever climbing everything in sight, he was (and still is) the adventurous one. He was also very social. Right from the time he was a baby he would smile a lot, soaking up the attention as he beamed with his sweet round cheeks at those around him.

During the pregnancy, my husband and I decided on the names Daniel or Michael if this baby was a boy, and Daniella or Michaela if it was a girl. But the moment he was born and we looked at his little face, we knew his name was Daniel. It was as if God had appointed this name for him. Daniel means, 'God is my Judge', a meaning that became increasingly appropriate when, years later, Daniel entered his adolescence. As things got tough with our son, we often grappled with what consequences to put in place. It was often easier to ask God to deal with it. This was neither passive nor punitive. I simply envisaged myself handing him over to God. I was giving him over to someone with more authority, to a loving and righteous Judge who is both just and merciful. Inviting God to have His way was reassuring to my heart as a mother. I knew God had the final say—and that was a good thing!

* * *

As Daniel grew, our hopes for him were high. He had a wild imagination, and loved to draw. He was also quite independent and liked to do things his way from an early age. I remember taking him for drawing lessons during a school holiday when he was around five years old. I dropped him off with his younger brother and when I returned an hour later with their lunch, the man running the programme called me over and said, "Daniel said he wanted to show me what he can do first before I teach him, and Daniel sat and drew what he wanted to draw." I did not mind so long as he was polite, which the man couldn't really fault him on; he'd just never met a kid who was so forthright.

Daniel could make friends with anyone and enjoyed getting people on board with an idea. He demonstrated leadership traits from a young age. Once, his younger brother went to a party, and the family, who were close friends of ours, invited Daniel along. When I picked the boys up, the mother who had organised the party called me over. Automatically I thought, *What now?* Instead, she told me how Daniel managed to keep ten kids entertained for two hours. He gave them instructions, led games and organised teams. This mother said it was the easiest party she ever had to host because he pretty much took over. He was only nine years old at that time.

By now we had three sons, my husband had started a business, and we were part of a large church which we attended weekly. We also had a small group of friends who we met with during the week. Life went on smoothly year after year, filled with work, school, and church. After nine years, we moved to a slightly smaller church, and two years later, we moved to an even smaller church where around one hundred people attended the service each week. We hoped it would be a good fit for the whole family.

So there we were, going to church as a family. My husband prayed and read the Word daily. I prayed and read the Word most of the time, although I can't say I was on fire in my spiritual walk. I had accepted Christ when I was nineteen years old and had a close relationship with the Lord which, depending on the difficulties in my life, ebbed and flowed. In short, I was in a comfortable relationship with the Lord in that we were settled in a church, we were serving there on the weekends, and work and home life were stable. Little did I know that this was going to change.

* * *

Daniel started high school and immediately proved to be popular with his peers. His teachers on the other hand had a love-hate relationship with him—they either loved or hated him. There was no middle ground. Daniel worked well with the teachers he liked and respected but he was not one to fake or hide his feelings. He struggled working in subjects he did not like.

He was fourteen when the true 'teenage years' started kicking in—that time when kids test their independence and push the limits of the boundaries their parents have set. It seemed as if overnight, parties and socialising with friends became his focus and we were relegated to the role of taxi drivers. We were fine with dropping him off and picking him up and although we were a little concerned, as the friendships he established tended to be more from school than church, what worried us more was the slow progression of change we were witnessing in his attitude—not so much towards us but definitely towards the faith he had grown up in. As a teenager he started to want to explore more of the things of the world.

Over time it became increasingly difficult to convince our son to attend church with us. We had been attending Saturday night services and afterwards, we would go out for dinner as a family. I remember in the beginning, we allowed Daniel to attend a couple of Saturday evening brithday parties. But even on other weeks, when we asked him if he was ready for church, he would stall, delay, and procrastinate almost to the point of us having to leave him behind if we were to get to church on time.

A few weeks of stalling eventually turned into him saying, "I don't feel like going." My husband would respond with, "What else is there to do here? You may as well come. We're going out afterwards." Sometimes Daniel would agree; other times he would come because his brothers asked him to. But it was obvious he was making no effort to fit in to church life at this time. The car rides were so long with him in the back seat, grumpy and sulking with his headphones on. He would pout all the way there, and while part of me worried that it was bringing the mood down in the car, the other part of me was just glad he was coming to church.

At church he would look down at his phone most of the time. He sat in the youth section with the other teenagers his age, looking miserable, like he had been dragged in there (which he had been) and there was no way he could pretend he wanted to be there. One of his greatest gifts and great curses is that this boy doesn't fake it! At home he complained that he didn't have friends at church and didn't feel connected to anyone there. That was hard to hear as a parent. Why couldn't he just make an effort to fit in?

Getting Daniel to church was a battle for ten long weeks of bribing, coercing and trying to 'sell' church to him. But eventually it was just easier to leave him at home because his attitude was so bad. Any mention about church or faith led him to shutting down the conversation or changing the subject.

"Church is boring," he would say.

"What do you mean church is boring?" I would ask in desperation, thinking that at least if I could get to the heart of the problem, maybe I could fix it.

"Well, we just sit there. I don't have friends. I'm not really learning anything." Daniel's responses were all truths that cut straight to my heart. I couldn't really offer any comeback to what he said as I know at that age, I felt similar feelings towards going to church.

There was nothing more we as parents could do or say. It was like holding onto the threads of a garment, that point where sentimentality meets the reality of the age of the garment; where something is so hard to let go of, but you realise it is not possible to hold onto either.

Maybe the father in the prodigal son parable felt this too. Maybe he did try to talk the prodigal out of taking his inheritance early. I can imagine him in despair saying, "What are you doing? You're going to waste your life. Stay! You don't know what you're missing out on! What there is for you here is so much better than what is out there in the world for you."

Certainly, those were the words that I wanted to say, wanted to shout. I was desperate to somehow sink them in to my son's mind. But it was like holding fine sand in an open palm in the wind. My son, just like the young man in the parable, had made up his mind. He would go so far as to make our lives difficult if we didn't let him have his way. With every step he took away from our faith, my head lowered in shame, and as I watched him walk down a path I would never even have thought was an option for him, it felt like my hopes and dreams for his life were going with him.

We struggled to know how to navigate this new stage of parenting. *Should we force him to come with us to church, or give him the space to choose his own path?* My heart yearned to see him happy and willing to be part of the church, but I also knew my boy, and without keeping his Christian connections I did not see what would attract him back. Besides, I wanted far more than just his body sitting in that church, fuming and rebelling; I wanted his heart to be present. But for that to happen, it had to be his choice.

It helped to remember my own prodigal journey in my late teenage years. I had attended church as a child with my grandparents, probably from the ages of ten to seventeen. I attended Sunday School weekly, prayed, and read my Bible daily, however every time there was an altar call, I felt the need to respond to God but I never really felt 'clean' or saved. Then around age eighteen, after finishing high school, I started to wander. I began to lose interest in my prayer times and in reading the Bible. There was a drift in my life, an attraction into the wider 'worldly' environment. I felt the pull of spending time with peers in the workplace and set out on a path which seemed more exciting to follow. Just like my son who slowly became disinterested in church or the things of God, I would make justifications, like, "Well it doesn't matter, because my parents didn't attend church." I ignored the inner conviction of the Holy Spirit and ignored the voice of God. Soon I gave in to sinful habits and lived in direct disobedience to the will of God.

Slowly I moved further from the faith. In fact, for about fifteen months I rejected everything to do with God. And it affected me. I think the further we move from the source of love and joy, the less we feel them in our lives. After about a year, I was in a depressed state. I started searching for answers but I simply did not know how to get back to God. Then, I got a call from a friend who I hadn't heard from in over a year. This friend convinced me to catch up for a coffee. Over steaming mugs of the strong brew my friend asked a simple question: "How are you doing spiritually?"

"Um … not so good," I replied. "I haven't been back to church."

This friend could read between the lines. She saw the fear and uncertainty that gripped my heart. It wasn't just that I had drifted from God. I was afraid that if I went back, I would not be loved, that I would not be welcome again because I had moved so far away.

"Well, nobody is going to care," she said. "Come back to church!"

Her words sat with me and called to me for another two weeks. Finally, I got up the courage to turn back to the people of God. I decided to go to a night service at the church I had attended when

I was younger. Thankfully, when I returned, even though the church had a new location, most things were the same as I remembered them, especially the pastors, and it was good to see some familiar faces. Fortunately, the young adults' group was flourishing, and there were plenty of others my age, so I didn't stand out the way I had been so terrified I would. The night I returned to church, I committed my life to the Lord. This time I was sure of my commitment. I felt free and clean and was thankful to have been given a second chance to be in a relationship with the Lord.

In contrast, my husband's journey was a lot more straightforward. He was saved at the age of thirteen. He attended Christian camps and had never missed reading his Bible daily or praying. He was part of the young adults' group at the church where I joined, was involved with the youth ministry, and played guitar as part of the worship band. While this was a blessing, it also made it much harder for him to understand our son's rebellion. This led to disagreements between us as to how to handle this stage of parenting.

One thing we could agree on was that we were in a battle with eternal consequences. The outcome of this battle would be an eternity with God or an eternity without God—and it involved someone we loved more than we loved ourselves. We knew we both wanted our son to choose the path that secured his future both in this life and eternity.

Neither of us wanted our son to take the long way around. As a mum, I didn't want squandered inheritances and pig pens for my boy. I wanted him to enjoy all that God had prepared for him. But I knew if my son wanted to leave the 'Father's house', he would. My hope was that if Christ had kept me safe during my prodigal journey, He would keep my son safe too.

2

DEALING WITH DISAPPOINTMENT

GOD DESIGNED FAMILIES AS A UNIT, TO move as a living organism. In families, more than in any other environment, what one member does or believes impacts everyone else. This is why our children's rebellion can feel like such a personal attack on our family unit. It's as if they are not only rejecting our faith—they're rejecting *us*.

Alongside the pain of this perceived rejection, when our families don't look like what we laboured and hoped for, disappointment comes. My greatest disappointment was primarily for my younger sons who had always looked up to Daniel. *What would all of this mean for them? How would their impressionable hearts be impacted?* Ultimately what this season exposed for us was that we were not operating in the unity God intended us to; we were thinking individualistically, and God wanted to bring us together so we could thrive as a team.

Holding a family together with a prodigal child in the mix is harder than it sounds. Daniel's journey consumed much of my attention, prayer and focus as we tried to get him back on track. It was difficult to focus on other things; this was uncharted territory for our family, and sometimes I needed to be reminded that I had two other sons who also needed me. However, I found that it was my marriage that began to feel the effects of having a prodigal in the home first. In fact, my husband and I spent months arguing, mostly about which one of us cared more about our child's spiritual state. I remember one argument in particular where my husband voiced the view that I didn't care because I did not try to force or convince our son to attend church.

"You're being too pushy and you are going to push him away!" I retorted.

"No, you are letting him get away with excuses!"

"He doesn't have friends! He doesn't have the connections in the church! You have to give him the space he needs to choose the right path for himself!"

These arguments seemed so unnecessary. I would contemplate and even wrestle with the idea that life would probably be easier if we weren't a Christian family. I would think, if we weren't Christians, these arguments would not even be happening! There would be no issue. We would be happier. We would have no stress about whether our son attended church. There'd be no pressure as parents about where our son was or how he was going, which caused me great angst. I wouldn't have to make pleasant excuses for his lack of interest in anything church-based. There would be no arguments about who cared more about his spiritual state, no trying to coerce or control him or beg him to come. We wouldn't be endlessly asking ourselves why he didn't come to church. There'd be no shame, no guilt. Instead, we would have an oblivious, enjoyable life.

Instead, the constant arguments between us continued. Some revolved around our parenting and the day-to-day struggles of raising a teenager, while others went right to the heart of our core beliefs. I questioned why we had to go through all of this conflict, all the assessing and analysing.

Truthfully, this journey caused us to question everything we believed about being Christians. We'd taken a lot for granted and were now forced to get to the nitty-gritty of our spiritual life. And we needed that. Everyone does, I believe. It made us really consider what was most important for us, the Christian habits we had become so accustomed to, the going to church, the praying, the attending small groups, but also our eternal legacy. We had to ask and wrestle with the real question: *What was the point?*

It had been difficult when Daniel was coming to church with us grudgingly. But now, every week that Daniel didn't come with us was difficult too. The twenty-five-minute drive to church was still filled with strife and debate about what more could we do to get Daniel to come back and attend with us. Even when we were in church I found myself particularly noticing those families with sons and daughters Daniel's age. *Why isn't our son here? What did we do wrong? What could we have done differently in the past few years?* This went on for months as we compared our 'failing' family to the other families who looked happy coming to church together. We felt like failures as parents.

We tried to avoid the topic and after months of making excuses about our son's absence at church, people mostly stopped asking. Occasionally they would enquire out of genuine interest, "Where is Daniel tonight?" and I would have to say that he was at a party, or at home, or with friends.

Even more disheartening was Daniel's total anti-God attitude. He didn't want to hear about our faith any more. For the first time, we experienced the stress of having a teenager unwilling to conform to what we knew or considered was best for him. I know the simple act of being in church was not the thing I should have been worried about. Of course, it was only church. But for me it was what the act represented. At that time, church was a large part of our lives. Daniel's rejection of that part of life brought out real insecurities in us as parents. We wanted him to be safe, to have friends who were doing well, to stay at home at night, to not want the things of this world. It really was a difficult time, one that could have ruined our marriage.

If there is one area in my life where I draw a line, one area that I will not allow the enemy a foothold, it is my marriage. For me the constant arguing and strife about not being the perfect example of a Christian family was taking a toll emotionally. One day, after one argument too many with my husband, I had had enough pretending. I was tired of carrying the burden of guilt, and I decided to share the 'secret' with our service pastor. That night, my husband and I had an argument and he decided not to go to the service. I drove to church alone, crying most of the way. There was no more hiding the pain. My eyes were red from crying and I was still sobbing when I walked through the front doors of the church. Seeing my grief, the pastor called me aside and we went to her office. She closed the door as I sat down. My shoulders were heavy with the weight of the burden I had been carrying for months, and my legs weak with fear. Sitting down opposite me, she asked in a kind voice, "What's happened? Why are you so upset?"

I looked down at my lap, scrunching the tissues she had placed in my hands. I gulped, trying to find words that would make sense. My pastor sat patiently and reassuringly with my silence and tears for what felt like the longest time. My gut swirled nervously as I tried to compose myself enough to speak coherently.

The office door was closed, it was private, and yet I felt so exposed. It seemed like an impossible thing to blurt out what I thought was my greatest weakness—my failure as a parent. But there was no turning back now. Finally, I swallowed hard, held back the tears, took a deep breath and just blurted out, "My son doesn't want to come to church and he won't be coming back for a while." The truth stunned me; it came out so fast. It was a truth we had hidden away for months, or at least not declared openly, and now it was spoken out loud it felt like a physical entity. *There,* I thought, *I told the truth, the blatant, ugly, dark, stark reality.* This was the burden I'd been carrying, the reason for months of arguing and strife.

And he won't be coming back for a while. That sentence rang in my ears. That was the truth that hurt the most. There was no way to know how long this would last.

I vividly remember that experience, the moment I spoke the truth out loud. I had confessed the 'secret'. I had let someone else know what was going on. And in that moment, the power of the enemy was broken. I cannot explain what happened spiritually, but something felt different.

Hidden things carry a weight that when spoken about can bring deliverance. The enemy loves it when we sit in our self-pity, our hopelessness, our shame or our guilt. He counts on us not wanting to be seen as weak and fragile, and the longer the enemy keeps us in darkness, the less light we are prepared to seek.

The Bible has a lot to say about the power of living in the light and the need for truth. 1 John 1:5-6 states, "This is the message which we have heard from Him and declare to you, that God is light and in Him is no darkness at all. If we say that we have fellowship with Him, and walk in darkness, we lie and do not practice the truth" (NKJV). Likewise, Daniel 2:22 says that God "reveals deep and hidden things; He knows what lies in darkness, and light dwells with Him."

Fortunately, my pastors at the time were very understanding. They prayed with me and encouraged me. Two other leaders shared their testimonies with me, stories that I would not have imagined or heard about had I not opened up about our situation. Their testimonies helped me to have hope that the God who saved them could do the same for my son.

One leader encouraged me to simply continue to attend church. He was a prodigal himself, but he saw his mother's faithfulness to God, watched her go to church every week, and heard her prayers for him. As a result, he eventually came back to a relationship with the Lord and was now actively involved in serving in church.

Although I hadn't considered leaving church, the shame I felt about my son's choice could have made it very easy for me to give up attending. It struck me that some parents attend for their children's sake. They set an example for their child to find faith by attending church, and when their children decide to walk a different path, the parents leave church. I knew that I was committed in my personal relationship with the Lord and that I did not want to leave. At church, I experienced grace, and was thankful that the pastors didn't attribute my child's choices to something I did or didn't do.

Convincing ourselves of that was much harder. As Daniel's parents and as spiritual stewards in this area of our lives, we felt we had failed. The questions were relentless. *How could this happen? What could we have done differently? Why was this happening to our family?* We had followed norms, done the 'right things', attended church, and yet now we had a prodigal son situation to deal with.

To make matters worse, I was a qualified counsellor working specifically in the field of child behaviour and personality types. I'd read all the books, run workshops and support groups, and even written courses based on the parenting approach we had adopted. I knew that as someone with a 'Type A' personality, I had a tendency to want to control my children, and I had worked hard over the years to find a more balanced approach that focused on our sons' unique personalities and offered age-appropriate opportunities for them to make their own decisions. We parented with positive affirmation, setting boundaries and giving clear directions. We had rejected a punitive approach, relying instead on appropriate consequences that we even gave them a choice in as they grew older.

To this day we still parent this way, but as Daniel rebelled more and more, self-doubt crept in. *Was this the right way? How could I give parents advice—especially leading into the teenage years—when my own child was being so rebellious? How could I continue to minister to others in my work and at church?*

I felt so unworthy and struggled with the thought that perhaps I could have done more. *Perhaps I should have been more spiritually-minded. Maybe I should have taught Daniel more from the Bible when he was younger*—the list goes on. Raising children is a big burden to bear, and so often we are left feeling disqualified!

As I listen to others talk about their prodigal journeys, I realise these are common feelings. Our children's choices cause us to feel like failures and we begin to believe that we are unqualified to minister to others. Consequently, we lose our confidence in church settings and don't feel like we can add any value, that having a prodigal somehow damages our credibility. It's an all-round humbling experience.

I was beginning to see, however, that Daniel's decisions were no longer in our control. That was a scary thing to come to terms with, but it was also freeing. There was no saying how long our son would choose to stay on his own path, and no way that I could make him change. Worst of all was the thought that he might never return. But as I wrestled with God as to how this could have all been avoided in the first place, the guilt and shame began to lift. I realised that all the wisdom we had accumulated over the years, all of our 'head-knowledge' and parenting theories were no longer sufficient; we needed revelation. We needed the breakthrough that only reliance on the Holy Spirit can bring. This really helped us as a family to set the foundation for the next stage.

First, however, I needed to realise that having a prodigal child does not mean I have lost my own righteousness! Rather than wallow in guilt, I had to trust deep within me that my righteousness is in Christ alone, in my personal relationship with Him. Romans 10:4 tells us that, "Christ is the culmination of the law so that there may be righteousness for everyone who believes." God does not measure us or judge us on our children or their faith choices; we are simply righteous because we are in Christ and He is righteous!

Of course, we can and should search our hearts and ask God if there is anything we have done that may have caused our child to take this path. He can show us if there is any area in our lives where we need to make adjustments or seek forgiveness if we have wronged our children. But ultimately, they choose their path of their own accord. If their decisions in life have drawn them away from their first love, our job is to stand in the gap and believe for them to return to the Father's house. We get to take the place of the 'middle man'! As parents we are tasked with being the agent of God's blessing and destiny in our children's lives. When we prioritise our intimacy with Him even while our children wander, our witness helps them experience God's heart for them.

After months of beating ourselves up about what we could or should have done differently, God revealed a similar truth to my husband. He brought to his attention the story in John chapter nine where Jesus healed a blind man on the sabbath. John 9:2-3 records it like this:

> *His disciples asked him, "Rabbi, who sinned, this man or*
> *his parents, that he was born blind?"*
> *"Neither this man nor his parents sinned," said Jesus,*
> *"but this happened so that the works of God might be*
> *displayed in him."*

Sometimes, there is no reason for a situation except that the glorious splendour and work of God might be displayed! Nevertheless, it took my husband much longer to accept that he was not at fault than it did me. But this verse helped bring a sense of assurance. We knew that God was using this passage of Scripture to let us know that He hears us when we call, and desires to answer us. This verse also confirmed for me that God would do a work in my son—that He would be glorified through this difficult journey. As the guilt and shame started to be lifted off us by the truth of God's Word, I was able to start taking authority over the situation in the name of Jesus. The blind man's story stirred my faith and I began to pray: "God, save my son so that Your name will be glorified."

As we did the hard work of keeping our marriage and family intact during these years, I learned that arguing and wrestling among ourselves is fruitless, but that wrestling and persevering in our faith and the things of God is worth it! As we grew into the united organism that God intended us to be, we saw God take what the enemy meant to use to divide and destroy, and turn it for good, ushering us into greater wholeness. We began to taste the fruition of Psalm 84:11-12 (NKJV):

> For the Lord God is a sun and shield; the Lord will give
> grace and glory; no good thing will He withhold from
> those who walk uprightly. O Lord of hosts, blessed is the
> man who trusts in You!

But there was the deeper issue of our own righteousness, and it called into question the faith we had always lived by. *What was it about my Christian life that was so unattractive to my son? What was it that he was pulling back from?* I found my own faith being challenged. I had to become certain about what I believed. *Was my faith worth it? How could I convince my son that Christianity was desirable when he couldn't be rationally convinced?*

The answer was that he—and I—needed more than belief. We needed to *experience* God for ourselves. My son couldn't be convinced to return to God. He needed to be wooed. But what was attractive enough to woo him back when his eyes were looking in a different direction?

A glimmer of hope appeared when I realised that God Himself was desirable! If I was to become more attractive to my son, I needed to be drawn into more of the likeness of God. I needed to discover a new level of intimacy with my own heavenly Father. I needed more of Jesus in *my own* life!

THE WAITING

- Distant from Home -

When he came to his senses, he said, "How many of my father's hired servants have food to spare, and here I am starving to death! I will set out and go back to my father and say to him: Father, I have sinned against heaven and against you. I am no longer worthy to be called your son; make me like one of your hired servants." So he got up and went to his father. But while he was still a long way off, his father saw him and was filled with compassion for him; he ran to his son, threw his arms around him and kissed him.

Luke 15:17-20

3

LETTING GO

IT HAD BEEN ABOUT FIVE MONTHS SINCE Daniel stopped attending church. Fear began to rise within me. Initially he wasn't too wild but he was pursuing a life very different from the one we had introduced him to and I thought to myself and even asked our pastor, "How far will he have to go before he comes back? How bad is this going to get? How low is he going to go?" The pastor listened graciously and responded calmly to my fears. She reassured me that any words he had heard in childhood would not be forgotten.

Isaiah 55:11 says:

So is my word that goes out from my mouth: It will not return to me empty, but will accomplish what I desire and achieve the purpose for which I sent it.

I knew that Daniel had heard the Bible as a child. He knew the truth about Jesus, and I had to trust in God's Word that those words Daniel had heard were not wasted, that the seed was, in fact, seed that could still be revived.

Even so, the fear was real. I remembered the verse of lament in Job 3:25:

> *What I feared has come upon me; what I dreaded has happened to me.*

Fear is a very powerful emotion. It can paralyse us or cause us to fight. Simply the thought of my son entering a dark world with no light to guide him scared me. I did not want that for him. Every parent wants the best for their child and here was mine refusing good, refusing peace, to go and follow a path that I knew could lead him to very dark places. I felt the loss of control in the situation.

I struggled with the thought that Daniel wasn't ready to make decisions—especially decisions without my guidance. I know this is a struggle that most parents with teenagers go through. Teenagers need to find their independence, but I never thought our son would seek independence without the guidance and counsel of God in his life. I feared he would take drugs and become addicted to them. I feared him drinking underage and all the irresponsible behaviour that might go along with that. Some of my fears did become realities.

The other issue for us was that we had determined early in our parenting journey that we would not use punishment as a means of shaping behaviour. This stood us in good stead, but there was an unexpected fallout from that approach. Knowing that he didn't need to fear punishment and that we'd rather hear than not know, Daniel shared freely what was going on in his life. Daniel is the talker in our family, which actually helped us a lot! He didn't try to hide where he was at from us. He didn't feel he needed to. That meant we always knew what he was getting into. On the other hand, it was hard to hear all the things he was trying—like weed. Daniel's openness left us open to one shock after another. It also left us feeling somewhat powerless. If our default response was not punishment, what else could we bring to the mix?

All I could do was pray, and trust God that He knew where and what my son was up to at all times and would keep him from harm. As I prayed, I sensed God assuring me that Daniel would be my greatest testimony.

* * *

We need to be aware of our fears and speak about them openly. If our fears are brought into the light, the enemy has no power to use them against us. If we talk about our fears, we can be better prepared to deal with them if they do happen. We can hopefully get reassurance and prayer from others. Job also experiences the weight of his fears. "For sighing has become my daily food; my groans pour out like water," he says in Job 3:24. When we become exasperated and weary we can trust that God hears, and pray that He will bring people around us to encourage us on the journey.

I learned to cling to all that Scripture says about bringing things into the open. Psalm 34:5 states, "Those who look to him are radiant; their faces are never covered with shame." And Ephesians 5:12-13 says, "It is shameful even to mention what the disobedient do in secret. But everything exposed by the light becomes visible—and everything that is illuminated becomes a light."

When we bring our fears and the 'negative' situations we are facing into the light, God is able to reveal more about His plan so that we have more understanding of what is truly going on.

We must never underestimate the power of simply holding on in faith. In Mark 5, Jesus was on His way to heal Jairus' daughter when, after being delayed, some people from Jairus' house brought news that his daughter was dead, and said he should not bother Jesus anymore. Jesus overheard their words and told Jairus: "Don't be afraid; just believe" (v 36). He speaks the same message to us today.

If I had remained focused on my fears of what might lie ahead for Daniel, I would have missed the bigger picture, and my prayers would have looked very different. They would have focused on merely a small part of the problem and not the bigger picture. Fear can do that. It can constrain our faith. But if we are going to move forwards, we must cast off the spirit of fear. God's Word assures us that we do not have a spirit of fear, but of power and of love and of a sound mind (2 Timothy 1:7). We can rest in Psalm 34:4 and declare, "I sought the Lord, and He answered me; He delivered me from all my fears."

REVELATION

As we learn to direct our attention to the Lord, I believe that God will give us the messages we need to hear in the moments when we most need them, and in the form that speaks most deeply to our hearts. During the period when we were struggling to keep our son in church and were arguing with him about his choices over the weekend, I got an image in my mind from the Lord. In this image, there was a thick rope, just like the twisted rope used in boating. This thick rope was tied around my son's waist, and I had one end of it in my hands. My son was facing in my direction and the more I tried to pull on the rope to get him to come back to me, the more the rope frayed. Eventually the rope frayed so much it broke totally. Then Jesus stood beside me, in this image, and said, "Let the rope go."

I argued, "I can't, Lord! I might lose him totally."

Jesus encouraged me again saying, "Let the rope go."

As I let go of the rope, Jesus said to my son in a gentle, calm, soft voice, "Follow Me," and Daniel immediately started walking towards Jesus (who was still standing next to me).

I held onto this image for the entire time of my son's prodigal journey—a journey that would last almost two years. It was an image that I prayed into, believed God for, and hoped to see become a reality. For me, it represented two things: Firstly and most importantly, relationship; and secondly, that Jesus would call my son and he would follow.

The relationship with Daniel was more important than being right or winning any argument with him. He knew he wasn't on the right path. He knew he was choosing to deny and defy us as parents. This image reminded me that if I was to continue to try to convince him, force him, and remind him of the error of his ways, the relationship could have been destroyed. The relationship was hanging on a thread. I had to give up trying to control my son or the thread could break. I had to 'let the rope go', give up using my strength, my parental knowledge and wisdom (which by this time had become seriously challenged) and let God be the One in total control. The image of letting go of the rope gave me faith that Jesus would call my son, that a day would come when Daniel would become God's child. That left me with one purpose and cause at this point: to maintain a good relationship with my son.

There was more to the image, though. It also made me realise the deep importance of my own relationship with Jesus. Jesus was there, standing with me. That was the key in this situation. I needed to stay close in my relationship with Jesus, God and the Holy Spirit. God knew I needed Him in this situation where I had no control. It was all up to Him, all up to faith and trust. It meant giving up on myself and my own works and following whatever God told me to do.

Through this process, I realised how little I had really been focusing on God and the ways of God before this happened. Now, maintaining my personal relationship and connecting with God became as important as my son's salvation. I could think all day on the reasons why my son chose to stray. But it didn't matter why. What mattered was how to deal with the situation. The questions that had haunted me about whether I could have prevented things and why our son had chosen the path he did, started to fade as I chose to remain close to God myself.

The further my son walked away, the more I found myself actually drawing nearer to God. No longer could I treat the Bible simply as a text book. I needed God to speak to me. I needed to cultivate the ability to hear His voice personally and intimately so I knew what He was saying about my situation. I needed to learn to listen on behalf of someone else. In desperation, my prayer times would be longer as I would sit and cry and call out to God, "God, please save my son! God, please protect him. Call him!"

TRAVAILING PRAYER

My son's prodigal journey was transforming the way I prayed. I soon discovered myself crying out to God all through the day or night. If I was driving in the car, I would talk to God about my son. If I was making coffee at home or checking emails during the day, I would wonder about him, and immediately I would turn towards God. I would just whisper a prayer, or pray in my mind.

I would love to say all my prayers were full of faith but at the start most of them were just desperation cries. There were also truly remorseful cries of repentance from my side: "I'm sorry, God, if there was anything I didn't do that You may have wanted me to do to make Your ways more real to my son when he was younger." Some prayers were just one line: "God, I know You're in control. I know You love Daniel and I know You love me." Some prayers were about my interaction with my son: "Help me know what I should say now. God, help me not to react badly to what I have just heard." Many prayers were for godly wisdom.

Eventually I grew strong in prayer. I got a sense that this journey could last two years, four years, or even longer. The thought of living in this day-to-day state of heartache, sometimes despair, constantly feeling battle-weary and powerless, was overwhelming. Despite the hope I had, this was a very real and intense spiritual battle. I wondered if there was a way to end this battle sooner rather than later. If so, I wanted the short-cut! Perhaps it was this motivation that God so kindly used to develop intercession and travailing prayer in me. As C.H. Spurgeon once said:

> *"Prayer pulls the rope below and the great bell rings above in the ears of God. Some scarcely stir the bell, for they pray so languidly. Others give but an occasional pluck at the rope. But he who wins with heaven is the man who grasps the rope boldly and pulls continuously, with all his might."*

PARTNERING WITH GOD

My relationship with God also changed as I began to see Him as a father, a loving father who did not reject me when I called out to Him. The more I confessed and cried out to Him, the more my heart opened to Him, and the nearer He drew. Only a father could understand this pain. Only a spiritual father could heal my emotional pain and take away my sense of failure.

I'd started to realise my relationship was also a partnership with God. He wanted me to lean more on Him, to depend on Him. He was my strength when I felt weak. God did not disappoint me. He was my lifeline. When I felt shameful and guilty, He was where I felt comforted and loved. I felt reassured that He could redeem any mistakes I may have made. He could fix this situation and turn it for good. He was in control, working things out. I was learning obedience. I was open to listening to Him for guidance, probably more than I had been in the past. I knew I may not be able to fathom or fully understand God and His ways, but I could fully depend on Him. Over time I found myself taking no spiritual experience for granted as I learned to talk freely and openly with God as a father and friend.

I also realised that the spiritual is just as real as the physical. Having a relationship with God is more than simply spending fifteen minutes in the morning or at night with Him and bringing our troubles or needs to Him. God is not confined to a time and place. He is everywhere! I was experiencing His nearness continually and I loved that I could talk to Him at any moment, knowing that He was a faithful and ever-present friend. I had been used to talking to God as my children grew up, but not as much or as often as I did during our journey with Daniel and in the years that have followed. I have found that as I press into God it has become easier to identify His presence, to feel close to Him, and to rely on Him. It really is only because of Him that we are able to have salvation from all our fears!

PRAYING THE SCRIPTURES

If (or rather, when) I felt afraid or discouraged or weary I would thank God for the image He had shown me and remind myself that Christ cared and was active in our lives. Part of this was letting my mind dwell on verses that encouraged my trust in Christ. I especially dwelt on the words of Jesus in John 6:44: "No one can come to me unless the Father who sent me draws them."

As I read that verse, I began to thank Jesus that He was the One who alone would call my son back.

Other scriptures reminded me that I was not alone in my intercession—Jesus was interceding for Daniel too! Romans 8:34 says:

Christ Jesus who died—more than that, who was raised to life—is at the right hand of God and is also interceding for us.

Hebrews 7:25 also became a favourite of mine:

Therefore He is able to save completely those who come to God through Him, because He always lives to intercede for them.

And I clung to the promise of John 6:45:

They will all be taught by God. Everyone who has heard the Father and learned from Him comes to me.

This was my hope—that my son who had been taught some of the Bible and knew about God the Father would come to know Jesus.

As I soaked myself in Scripture and turned the promises of God into prayer for my son, my own faith was strengthened. Each of those verses, along with my vision, reminded me that Christ had a plan for my son and a power to save him beyond anything I could do! I was learning to stop trusting in my own strength and release control of the situation. I was learning to let go of the rope.

4

LOVING UNCONDITIONALLY

ONE OF THE MOST CONCERNING CHANGES IN our home when Daniel was going his own way was that the conversations in our home grew more tense. My sweet and smiley child had been replaced by a mean, insolent, argumentative and reclusive teen whose innocence was gone. No longer were we talking to Daniel about his dreams and plans for the future or asking him what he was trusting God for. Instead, the questions became: "Where were you? Were you drinking last night? What drugs have you tried? What drugs are your friends taking?"

A whole other world had opened up and we were having to have conversations about things that, as a Christian parent, I had hoped to avoid. It felt like we had been placed on opposing sides of a battlefield I didn't want to be on. The words 'no' or 'you can't' or 'you shouldn't' inevitability escalated the tension, leaving us with a nasty mess. Most of the time I would default to 'maybe' (which he remarked to his brother usually meant no!) accompanied by a whole lot of asking God to intervene or turn something around without me having to stir up a conflict.

As parents, the word 'no' often feels like a safe response. We hope that one word will be enough to stop our children's behaviour. But it doesn't take temptation away, and it doesn't have the power to change a mind that is set on things that are not of God. The season of straying for a prodigal is a time of wanting what the flesh wants; for a parent it needs to be a time of seeking what God wants and of learning to love as He loves.

A few months after my vision of letting go of the rope, God told me I was to love Daniel unconditionally. As any parent of a prodigal knows, that's not always easy!

What does it mean to love unconditionally? It's precisely that act of letting the rope go. It's giving up on the struggle to maintain control of someone else and their actions. It's loving someone despite their choices—or even in the midst of their choices. This was the plan God had for me on this journey: to love my son unconditionally. It was a plan that caused me to draw nearer to God.

There is a beautiful verse in Hosea 11:4 which reads:

I [God] led them with cords of human kindness, with ties of love. To them I was like one who lifts a little child to the cheek, and I bent down to feed them.

How do I even begin to imagine what love is, especially the type of love God has for each of us, His children? He is the perfect example of a father. Consider all He did for Israel in the Old Testament and they still disobeyed Him. They wanted things their way even when it wasn't in their best interests. God warned them that having kings would not be good for them but they would not listen, so God gave them what they asked for—other kings to rule over them. Some were good kings who pleased God. Others were evil kings whose ways were not aligned to God at all.

In the same way, I eventually had to accept our son's choice not to attend church. I would invite him, but I would no longer get angry with him if he said 'no'. I also did not remind him of his shortcomings. If he shared a story of something that happened that affected him negatively, I refrained from my usual comeback, "Well if you went to church or served God this would not happen. Life would be good if you came back to God." Instead, I had to choose my words carefully. I tried really hard to listen more so that I didn't overreact or speak from a place of judgement.

Learning to love Daniel in this way strengthened our parent-child relationship. It kept communication open between us. He knew home was a safe place, that I wasn't going to 'lose it' if he told me something that may have shocked me or disappointed me, and that no matter what, I loved him anyway.

OUR RESPONSES

I remember one day, about nine months before our son started to come back to faith, when I realised how much I had learned about unconditional love. Daniel was in a very depressed state by this time. He was miserable. He had an appointment with a psychologist who specialised in anxiety and depression but he was resistant to seeking help. The psychologist welcomed him into the office and I waited in the waiting room. After about thirty minutes I got called into the meeting. My son's face was expressionless as I entered. I sat next to him on the couch facing the psychologist. Based on the few questions she was asking him, with me in the room, and Daniel's short snappy 'yes' or 'no' answers, I could tell no rapport had been built and this session was a total waste of time and money. He showed very little interest in being there and the atmosphere in the room, despite being bright and airy with the sun coming in the window, felt chilly and wintery.

I tried to lift the mood a little by smiling and prompting Daniel to answer in full sentences or with a little more detail but my presence did little to change the dynamic and eventually I just sat with unease and a tinge of insecurity about my parenting. How could I have raised someone so cold and unfeeling? His stone-faced expression was certainly not one I would like to be sitting across from. I felt embarrassed by his behaviour and tried to reassure myself that as a professional, the psychologist would have seen this before, *surely?*

Clearly she had not been able to build up any rapport with Daniel, and it appeared she didn't relish the challenge. Still, I think even her own identity could not withstand what was to come next. Bringing the session to a close, she asked, "So, Daniel, what is one thing you would like to take out of today's session?" *One good thing about today's session?* Blank-faced, Daniel looked her straight in the eyes and replied, "Nothing. I don't think I got anything out of this."

At that, the psychologist stood up abruptly, walked to her door and told us we could leave. She said to Daniel, "I hope that one day you can have respect," along with a few other sentiments that I failed to hear in the moment. She walked out ahead of us and both Daniel and I noticed she was emotional as she walked to a back room.

I left with a mixture of emotions. I felt embarrassed. I was a little angry, shocked at how the session had ended, and disbelieving that this was actually happening. *Did my son just break the psych?*

Daniel left the office and headed out of the building. I remember going to pay for the session, then heading towards the main glass door. I could see Daniel waiting for me on the other side. He was facing the door and as I approached him, I saw his eyes get wider and wider. I'm sure he could sense my displeasure with his behaviour in the office only minutes before, and he looked afraid. My normal approach would have been to ask in a judgemental, accusatory way, "What were you thinking? Why did you do that?" Instead, I made the choice not to respond in my usual way.

As I came to the door and saw his expression of fear, I understood that he did know he had done something wrong. I realised I had to choose whose side I was going to take. Was I going to side with the psychologist who clearly did not connect with my son in a meaningful way and who we were not going to have any relationship with going forward? Or was I going to choose my son? Would I give him the benefit of the doubt that he still had some warmth, some good, some respect deep inside him?

In that moment, I chose unconditional love. Despite feeling angry, I chose my son! Yes, he had just cost me money. Yes, I was embarrassed by his bad behaviour and disrespect towards another adult. Yes, my mind was churning as I grappled with my own feelings of disappointment and self-judgement about my parenting skills. But I made a conscious choice to love. Putting all that aside, I grabbed the handle to swing the door open.

He was quiet as I joined him outside the building. My expression was still firm. But we walked a few steps next to each other, and then, as we got about ten metres from the building, I just burst out in laughter. I said, "I can't believe we just got kicked out of her office! That was a bit unprofessional don't you think?"

"Oh, Mum," Daniel replied. "It was *so* bad! I'm sorry if I wasted your money."

"It's okay," I said, "but we do need to keep working on finding you someone you can relate to." I then got the chance to explain that I felt embarrassed, and he was able to talk about what he felt. He made a comparison between sessions he'd had with other professionals, and we talked easily and freely about what good help looks and feels like.

As I reflect on why I kept my stern expression at first, I think the truth is, I wanted to see how he would react. I guess part of me still wanted him to know that what just happened in the office wasn't a joke. Maybe I was still second-guessing my choice. *There should be consequences for bad behaviour, shouldn't there? Was showing him unconditional love at this time the right thing? Surely, I should be making him 'pay' for embarrassing me, making him suffer some consequence for wasting my time and money?*

But unconditional love meant that I chose to back him up even though he did, in this instance, take the cool attitude a bit too far. I was standing with my son, even if he didn't deserve it—in fact he probably deserved a berating for his behaviour. Instead, I chose to come with a disarming approach and gave him time to tell his side of the story. After all, I wasn't in the room for the first thirty minutes of the session. By giving him the benefit of the doubt, I could show him that, although I did not agree with his behaviour, I did have his back. I let him know that I would be on his side no matter what.

Unconditional love put my thoughts and emotions aside and allowed me to continue to protect, trust, hope, and love my son even if he had wronged me or embarrassed me. I trusted that he was still good. I felt such peace. And in that instant, I knew what it felt like when God forgives us. He keeps no record of wrongs and does not stay angry. Likewise, I could not stay angry with my son. I sought no consequence or revenge; I simply chose to accept him. Love swept over me and not only healed my own emotions from that disastrous session, but helped me build a stronger bridge with my son.

The Bible teaches us that not only does God love, but He *is* love. And His love is *agape* love, the kind of love that will lay everything down for the one it loves. And so, this became another area where, in helping me respond to my son, God grew me spiritually, teaching me what it means to love unconditionally. It was in God's Word that I found myself tutored in how to love my son in practical ways. I found myself guided by 1 Corinthians 13:4-7:

> *Love is patient, love is kind. It does not envy, it does not*
> *boast, it is not proud. It does not dishonour others, it is*
> *not self-seeking, it is not easily angered, it keeps no record*

*of wrongs. Love does not delight in evil but rejoices with
the truth. It always protects, always trusts, always hopes,
always perseveres.*

You cannot control someone if you love them unconditionally. This is how God loves us. He didn't place robots or puppets in the Garden of Eden. He created individuals with total freedom and provided them with options, including the wrong one, so that they always had the choice to obey or not. God's love is a love that gives the gift of free will. I had to come to a place where, even though it was terrifying, I chose to give Daniel his freedom. I found great comfort in 1 Peter 4:8:

*Above all, love each other deeply, because love
covers over a multitude of sins.*

I didn't approve of my son's behaviour, but I learned to love him and to focus, not on the individual behaviours, but on Daniel's heart. I found that with God's help it was possible to stop fighting about little things and hand them over to the One who loved Daniel even more than I could. As it says in Psalm 86:15:

*You, Lord, are a compassionate and gracious God, slow to
anger, abounding in love and faithfulness.*

Did I like the music he listened to during that time? No. Did I like the people he hung out with? No. Did I approve of the drinking and partying and staying out? No, I despised it all, but I learned to pray a lot despite it. I prayed for God's intervention, for God to protect Daniel, for God to stand by His promises, and especially for God to soften my boy's heart.

Gradually, I saw the bigger picture. I realised that the journey wasn't only about our son. As is so often (or perhaps always) the case when God allows us to walk through difficult times, He has a plan that affects everyone. Much of this prodigal journey wasn't about what Daniel was going through, but about me experiencing the faithfulness of God and having my own story of growth.

I look back now and joke about 'my poker face'. I really am no good at keeping a secret or telling a lie because my face gives me away most of the time. But when my son would tell me things that would stir me up, my challenge was to control my reaction. I would ask myself, is he just saying this to get a reaction or to start an argument? Often, the answer was yes.

I also found we could have deep discussions while we were driving somewhere. Daniel would talk in the car. As I took control of my outward reaction, he felt safe to tell me almost everything he did. This meant I had to work very hard on looking straight ahead and breathing deeply so I didn't just fly off the handle or start to lecture or berate him for his stupid choices or behaviour. Instead, as he talked I would sit silently, praying for God's grace and wisdom about what to say and how to respond with love. I had to realise that there was no point in responding with a lecture. Countless times my natural instinct was to say, "Well that was a stupid decision," or, "How could you do that? That's so bad!" That's when I had to revert to gentleness and loving grace. I had made the decision to respond in a self-controlled and loving way. In the words of Proverbs 15:23, "A person finds joy in giving an apt reply—and how good is a timely word!"

Daniel already knew that he was away from God and that his actions did not please me, so there was little I could say to make him feel worse. I chose all the time to rather give a gentle answer and wait before reacting. Proverbs 15:1 tells us why this is so important.

A gentle answer turns away wrath, but a
harsh word stirs up anger.

There is a difference between our wisdom and God's wisdom. James 3:17 explains that the wisdom that comes from heaven is "first of all pure; then peace-loving, considerate, submissive, full of mercy and good fruit, impartial and sincere."

I had to seek His wisdom—after all, He created my son and He knew him better than I ever could. Often, we feel the need to justify our faith to our children, or attempt to convince them of our beliefs using argument and intellect, but I have learned to leave that to God. As Luke 21:14-15 says:

> *Make up your mind not to worry beforehand how*
> *you will defend yourselves. For I will give you words*
> *and wisdom that none of your adversaries will be*
> *able to resist or contradict.*

OFFERING FORGIVENESS

Unconditional love is tied to forgiveness. When our children do something that requires discipline, it's important to follow through. I realised, however, that after disciplining my child he still felt he needed to earn back my trust, or prove himself in that area before I could reward him. I'm sure most parents relate—we so easily raise past issues as a reminder for them not to do that behaviour again, or find ourselves joking about a previous misdemeanour. Maybe you've even heard your child say, "Can't we just move past that?" The essence of love is that it doesn't remind us of our past, it doesn't reinforce guilt and shame. Love wipes the slate totally clean! Love says, "I accept you. I will try to help you find another way." In the words of 1 Corinthians 13:5, "Love ... keeps no record of wrongs."

ALLOWING CHOICE

Sometime after his prodigal experience, I asked my son, "What do you think we did to help you come back to God?" I was a little taken aback when he replied, "You gave me a choice." As most parents know, that's a difficult thing to do. It was only by God's grace that I was able to give my son a choice. Only by His strength could I let go of the rope, the control, and let myself be ruled by love, not fear.

Giving Daniel a choice required me to lower my expectations. I had to acknowledge he was going to make bad choices, act foolishly, and waste precious time. This wasn't easy. As I released my expectations of my son, I needed to raise my expectation of God and rely on Him to redeem what He had created.

I remember Daniel asking me if he could go to a particular event. I really didn't want him to go but I knew that by saying no I would only create a dispute which would lead to an argument. So I said yes, but then prayed and left the situation up to God. Two days before the event was to take place, it was cancelled. Once again, God fought the battle for me, answered a mother's prayer, and protected my son. Ephesians 6:12 says:

> For our struggle is not against flesh and blood, but
> against the rulers, against the authorities, against the
> powers of this dark world and against the spiritual
> forces of evil in the heavenly realms.

We can easily find ourselves turning against our prodigal child and entering into conflict with them when we operate in the flesh instead of recognising the spiritual dynamics that are at work. But God's Word says that our battle is not against flesh and blood! I ultimately realised that the battle we were facing was not with our son, but with the enemy and his schemes. Satan knows the calling on our children's lives. He sees that they are made in the image of God and actively conspires to bring them down. God, on the other hand, wants the best for our children! He longs for them to prosper and live, even more than we do! Understanding that Daniel was being attacked by the enemy, made me realise the incredible calling on my son's life. In prayer, I was coming against these principalities and powers that wanted to destroy him.

The enemy has no love for our children, but God loves them fiercely and unconditionally, and His love always triumphs over the darkness. As parents, we are the closest representation of God for our children. When we become conduits of God's love, relentlessly choosing to draw near to them despite their ugly behaviour, we give them a glimpse of the truest love: the love of their heavenly Father.

5

LEANING ON GOD

IENJOY THE MOUNTAINS, ESPECIALLY WHEN THEY are covered in snow. My husband and boys really enjoy skiing and snowboarding. One night, I dreamt of a snow-covered mountain. There were many different ski tracks on the mountain and Daniel was skiing down one of them. Then I heard in the dream, "All the paths lead to Jesus." I woke up with the words still clearly in my mind, "All paths lead to Jesus." I believe God confirmed in this dream that no matter what path my son took, he was going to be saved. God would not let Daniel go!

The Bible is full of reminders that God can talk to us through our dreams. In Genesis 37 Joseph had dreams about his future. When he told his brothers what he had seen, they became even more jealous of him, but his father wisely kept the matter in mind, knowing that dreams can be prophetic. This was the case for Joseph. The jealousy of his brothers caused them to sell him into slavery but after some time (and many trials) Joseph's destiny was fulfilled and his dreams from earlier years became reality.

Dreams often foretell blessing, but they can also contain warnings or give directions. In Matthew 2 we read that after the birth of Jesus, Mary's husband was specifically warned and directed by an angel who appeared in a dream saying, "Get up . . . take the child and his mother and escape to Egypt" (v 13). Likewise, after the death of Herod, Joseph was directed by an angel in a dream to go to the land of Israel and settle in Nazareth in Galilee.

Knowing what the Bible teaches about dreams, I felt reassured after my own dream of the snow-covered mountains. It was a picture that connected so specifically to our family, and it enabled me to continue to hope. Informed by my dream, I began to pray, "Thank You, God, that any path my son takes leads him to Jesus."

* * *

I wasn't the only one who received dreams at this time. Around two o'clock one morning, I woke to Daniel crying out from his room, "It's so dark! Help me, help me! It's so dark!" Running into the bedroom, I found him shaking and reaching into the air. When I asked what happened, he said he had a bad dream. "I was in a very dark place. I couldn't see anything at all."

I was frightened too, seeing how scared he was. Trying to reassure him (and myself), I sat next to him and gently spoke to him: "Daniel, it's okay. You're safe. Shhh … calm down, it's okay." I didn't know what to do, but I knew I needed to pray with him, and I also felt strongly that I needed a Bible, so I told him, "Wait here. I'll be back."

"Why? Where are you going?" he asked. "Stay with me!"

"I'll be right back," I answered.

"No, I'll come with you," Daniel responded frantically. "I don't want to be alone." My fifteen-year-old independent son was grabbing onto my elbow like a small child. He would not let go as he lifted himself out of bed and stuck close behind me as we went to another room and grabbed the Bible from the side table.

"What are we going to do now?" Daniel asked.

"We're going to read it," I said as we walked back into his room and sat down on his double bed. "We'll just read a few verses, because I don't know what's happening. I don't mind if you don't want to read, but I think I should."

I had no specific scripture in mind so I literally held the Bible in my hands and let it fall open. The page opened to John's Gospel, and I calmly began to read a verse out loud. Daniel had his phone torch on, and as I stopped reading, he took the Bible from me and kept reading further, a few more verses on his own, while I sat next to him. "I really should read this more," he said when he had finished. "I feel better, I have more peace now." I prayed silently over him until he said, "It's okay now. You can go to your bed." Giving my son a hug, I left his room.

* * *

The next morning when I mentioned the incident to my husband it occurred to me that maybe Daniel had taken drugs and had a bad reaction. My husband, who had slept through the whole event, exclaimed, "What?! I prayed that God would show Daniel what it is like without Him in his life. I prayed he would experience what separation from God is like!"

Later that morning when Daniel got up, we asked him about drugs but he was adamant he hadn't taken any. Then we shared what his dad had prayed for him, and what that dream might have been about. Daniel didn't read the Bible again until after he was saved, but I believe that night he got a firsthand experience of what separation from God meant. It was a significant moment in his journey of eventually coming back to God.

THE FAITH OF OTHERS

While God was working through dreams, He was also working through the prayers of other believers. In the eighteen months that my son rejected our faith, I broke down more often in church than I had in the past twenty years of being in church! One occasion that stood out to me was when a woman in church, after noticing me crying, asked, "What's the matter?" I replied tearfully that I was still trusting God for my son to come back to Jesus. At that moment she stopped and prayed for Daniel, specifically that he would meet more Christians, that more believers would cross his path.

When my sense of guilt and shame was finally replaced by desperation, I began reaching out to ask others to pray. Sometimes I asked them to pray for something specific. Other times I simply said, "I want my son to come back to the Lord," and asked them to come into agreement with me. It didn't matter how intense my prayer was or how long. I simply needed others to stand with me, and to encourage me with a word or a verse to build up my faith.

Being able to admit that my son was on an alternative path was a key to this becoming a testimony. If we had been stuck in our pride, this experience would not have been able to bring glory to God. If no one knew about our struggle, how could my son's journey ever become part of my testimony of a faithful God who delivers us from all our troubles? It was by being open that his story led to a bigger story of God's deliverance and love.

PROMPTED BY THE SPIRIT

I also learned to be open to the promptings of the Spirit. On one particular day, when I was working from home, I left my home office and went into the kitchen to prepare myself some lunch. Pouring hot water into my cup of coffee, I was suddenly overcome with emotion and out of nowhere, I got a pain in my stomach. It wasn't a stabbing pain—more like a nervous sensation or an ache in the core of my being. I started to cry. Abandoning my coffee and the lunch I had prepared, I headed upstairs to get my Bible. I had no idea what to do with all the emotion I was feeling. As I cried and asked God what was going on, I was reminded of Romans 8:25-27:

> *If we hope for what we do not yet have, we wait for it*
> *patiently. In the same way, the Spirit helps us in our*
> *weakness. We do not know what we ought to pray for,*
> *but the Spirit himself intercedes for us through wordless*
> *groans. And He who searches our hearts knows the mind*
> *of the Spirit, because the Spirit intercedes for God's people*
> *in accordance with the will of God.*

In his book, *I Give You Authority*, Charles Kraft aptly describes intercession as, "…an intense kind of praying in which we lay hold of God's faithfulness and promises in regard to something that concerns us greatly." That's what I was experiencing! The feeling in my stomach continued over three days. It would come in waves, and I would drop everything and pray in the Spirit for up to two or three hours. I had a strong sense to pray with all my might, all my faith and as the Holy Spirit directed.

On the second day, I was emotionally and physically drained from all the crying and praying. I felt that I could not go on praying at this level of intensity. That afternoon, I was on my porch listening to a Christian song and still crying out to God when He said to me by the Holy Spirit, "Look up!" I looked up in the direction of the sky and He showed me an army of angels! One by one, yet more angels were joining the cohort. I felt the Holy Spirit say, "For every prayer that has been prayed, for every person that has prayed, an angel is added to this army."

As I meditated on this vision, I started to thank God for every person who had prayed for our son, for everyone who had held him in their prayers. I thanked Him for the power of intercession and for allowing me to feel such emotion in prayer. The Bible tells us that no tear goes unnoticed by Him. In fact, the psalmist said, "Record my misery; list my tears on your scroll—are they not in your record?" (Psalm 56:8).

Every murmur, groan, or sentence we pray moves heaven into action. The image of this angel-army helped me to love prayer because it gave me confidence that our prayers have an immediate effect. I learned through this experience that when things get intense, the battle is getting close to being won!

We see this principle play out in Daniel chapter 10 where for three weeks, Daniel mourns as he prays. At the end of that time, he sees a vision of a man dressed in white linen who says in verses 12-14:

> *Do not be afraid, Daniel. Since the first day that you set your mind to gain understanding and to humble yourself before your God, your words were heard, and I have come in response to them. But the prince of the Persian kingdom resisted me twenty-one days. Then Michael, one of the chief princes, came to help me, because I was detained there with the king of Persia. Now I have come to explain to you what will happen to your people in the future, for the vision concerns a time yet to come.*

Hearing these words, Daniel bowed his face to the ground, then said,

> *I am overcome with anguish because of the vision, my lord, and I feel very weak. How can I, your servant, talk with you, my lord? My strength is gone and I can hardly breathe. (vv 16-17)*

In the following verses we read:

The one who looked like a man touched me and gave me strength. "Do not be afraid, you who are highly esteemed," he said. "Peace! Be strong now; be strong." When he spoke to me, I was strengthened and said, "Speak, my lord, since you have given me strength." (vv 18-19)

Though Daniel had to wait to receive the answer to his prayers, the truth was, that answer was put into effect from the moment he started to pray. This encouraged me to continue in prayer. I thanked God for strengthening me through that vision and giving me fresh hope.

By the third day, after experiencing the depths of intercessory prayer, the groaning, the pouring out of my heart, and expressing my desires for the situation, I knew that there would be a good end to my son's story. I didn't feel the need to pray or cry as much. I had a strong sense of peace that the job was done and God would lead him home. It was only a few months after that intense intercessory period that God made a path back to Himself, and my son began to come home.

During this time of deep intercession, my husband was also praying. He would go for long bike rides, and it was on one of these rides that, led by the Holy Spirit, he asked God in desperation, "Even if you have to send a girl, let him come back to you!" This was an interesting prayer, as my husband always joked with my son that he couldn't have a girlfriend until he was twenty-five. Whether or not this was God's way of preparing my husband for what was to come next, I don't know, but it was indeed through a relationship with a girl that my son would be restored to a relationship with God as his Saviour and heavenly Father.

THE RETURN

- Coming Back Home -

The son said to him, 'Father, I have sinned against heaven and against you. I am no longer worthy to be called your son.' But the father said to his servants, 'Quick! Bring the best robe and put it on him. Put a ring on his finger and sandals on his feet. Bring the fattened calf and kill it. Let's have a feast and celebrate. For this son of mine was dead and is alive again; he was lost and is found.' So they began to celebrate. Meanwhile, the older son was in the field. When he came near the house, he heard music and dancing. So he called one of the servants and asked him what was going on. 'Your brother has come,' he replied, 'and your father has killed the fattened calf because he has him back safe and sound.' The older brother became angry and refused to go in. So his father went out and pleaded with him. But he answered his father, 'Look! All these years I've been slaving for you and never disobeyed your orders. Yet you never gave me even a young goat so I could celebrate with my friends. But when this son of yours who has squandered your property with prostitutes comes home, you kill the fattened calf for him!' 'My son,' the father said, 'you are always with me, and everything I have is yours. But we had to celebrate and be glad, because this brother of yours was dead and is alive again; he was lost and is found.'

Luke 15:21-31

6

TURNING AROUND

IT WAS THE YEAR OF MY SON'S junior high school formal. Daniel was struggling with depression, and although he was on medication, he still did not want to do anything social, especially attend his school formal. But the formal was a compulsory event, so we discussed this with the head of his year group, who was a very understanding person and really 'got' Daniel, and she arranged for him to leave as soon as the main formalities were over.

We received a call around eight o'clock that evening to say that Daniel could be picked up at the hall. My husband and I arrived about twenty minutes later to find Daniel standing outside with the teacher and a girl we hadn't seen before. He got in the car as quickly as he could and did not talk much on the way home. We asked the normal questions like, "How was it?" to which he replied, "Awful." And in that way we kept driving home.

Around nine-thirty, my husband and I were watching a movie when Daniel sheepishly came into the lounge room and asked if we could drop him off at an after-party. He explained that a group of kids were going to someone's house after the formal and the girl we had seen outside with Daniel when we picked him up had been texting him asking him to come.

My husband and I looked at each other and asked him whose house the party was at. When we heard that the party was at the home of some pastors who attended our church, we jumped off the couch and could not get him into the car fast enough. We were so excited that he wanted to go, especially considering that just an hour before he had not wanted to be at anything social. We drove him to the after-party, came home and finished our movie, before driving out for the fourth time that night. It was close to midnight when we picked him up, and although he was tired, he was more talkative this time. On the way home we heard all about who was there and how they all sat around in a spa pool. He even suggested we get one at our house.

About a month later Daniel introduced us to the girl as his girlfriend. We were so relieved when we heard that she was a Christian and from a Christian family. Daniel started attending youth group with her on Friday nights, and she attended church with our family. It was a relief knowing where he was on the weekend, especially after he got his driver's licence!

My son's transformation, especially mentally, was almost immediate. He spoke more positively in general, and even started inviting friends to youth group and church, and taking some along with him. We were overjoyed when he began a fresh relationship with the Lord. It was such a relief for my husband and I to see our son make such a turnaround. We thanked God for His faithfulness and for answering our prayers. Our son was now saved and on the right track again. But Daniel's commitment to staying on that track would certainly be tested.

* * *

It was two years later, during the week of Daniel's final high school exams when I walked into his room to find him crying. "Oh honey, what's wrong?" I asked. "She doesn't want to be my girlfriend anymore," he replied through sobs. "She told me it's over." A week before exams! I was shocked and stunned. I wanted to cry with him. Daniel hadn't seen much of his girlfriend the previous week; she had gone away on a family holiday and he was studying for exams. But this was the real test. Was his faith dependent on another person in his life? I had enjoyed having peace back in the family, and we had enjoyed seeing him happy again. Was this life-altering news about to bring destruction?

But no! Actually, it was wonderful. My son was devastated and broken-hearted of course, but finally he had a deep, personal relationship with God the Father, and a close relationship with Jesus Christ that would carry him through this challenge and any future challenges. He was, and is today, a child of God. It was amazing to witness. I saw firsthand how, when someone truly has a relationship with Jesus, they can survive storms, deal with injustices, and know their redemption is secure. Daniel's faith wasn't because of someone else, and it wasn't someone else's faith. It was his own revelation.

By God's grace, Daniel had received an early offer to university, so we knew he could get into his course even if he didn't do so well in those final exams. For the next week, however, God helped him to control his emotions. When he went to school to sit the exams, he would arrive as close to the time as possible so that he could walk straight to a desk and avoid seeing his ex-girlfriend. It was a tough four weeks as he studied through tears and faced the emotional and mental challenge of a breakup on top of the pressure of exams. In the end, Daniel successfully sat every exam and did well enough to get an even better university offer!

* * *

A few weeks after the breakup, Daniel decided to get water baptised at church. Knowing the church leaders normally asked people to share a short testimony before their baptism, we asked Daniel, "Have you prepared? What are you going to say?"

He started, "Well, that we are all sinners and that people should follow Jesus."

We listened and then replied, "Mmm … yes, you could say that, but it should be a personal story about you." It was still two weeks before his baptism so we left him to prepare his speech.

The night of his baptism at church he stood up with two other people on stage and shared his declaration of faith. "I'm publicly proclaiming that I'm a Christian because God has changed my life. I was on the highway to hell, but now I'm here. I'm so happy and it's all because of Him." His few words summed up his journey, but they didn't give insight into the enormous war that went on behind closed doors and in the private battlefields of prayer.

I had told Daniel before we left home that I wouldn't embarrass him, but as he was coming out of the water that night, I sobbed tears of joy, celebration, and relief. With a heart full of thanks, we gave glory to God that the battle for our son's salvation had been won!

After the baptism, we went out to dinner as a family and Daniel invited a friend from church who had also gone to high school with him. During the meal, the boy remarked on the transformation that he had witnessed in Daniel at school over the past two years. It was a testimony to the life-changing decision our son had made, and to the goodness and power of God to bring home a prodigal child.

It was so wonderful to talk with Daniel about the things of God again, to hear him ask questions about the Bible and to see him watching Christian evangelist videos in his search for deeper knowledge. As Daniel's questions about faith came out, often at the dinner table, my youngest son would often say, "Oh no, are we going to talk about God again?" What a great problem to have!

One night I was recovering from back surgery while my husband and boys were outside in the spa pool (yes, we did buy one!). As I listened to the Christian music being played through the speaker-system, and heard the talking and laughter, all I could do was give thanks to God once again for the miracle of Jesus and His transforming power in our family's life.

7

ESTABLISHING A SECURE FUTURE

OUR SON'S RETURN FROM HIS PRODIGAL JOURNEY wasn't sudden. It was a slow process, and I could not really tell you a time or day that it occurred. But I do remember how he started being drawn back to God, how he became interested once again in spiritual things. Eventually the desires of the flesh lost their hold, and he wanted to be in church or at Bible studies, mixing with other devoted Christians more. All I know is that the outcome of all the prayers and drawing of the Holy Spirit is this: he now walks in a new life with Jesus.

God does not forsake the lost. We must remember that the Bible tells us in Luke 19:10: "For the Son of Man came to seek and to save the lost."

Whatever our hopes and dreams are for our children, it is important that we remember how much more the Father who formed them and created them has plans for them. We love them, but there is One who loves them even more. Therefore we can rest securely knowing that

God's plans are far bigger than we can often fully comprehend and that He is actively working to see them fulfilled.

Today, Daniel openly witnesses to his friends and seeks out people to discuss the things of God with. My ongoing prayer for him is from Ephesians 1:17-19, that he will hear the voice of the Holy Spirit day by day:

> *I keep asking that the God of our Lord Jesus Christ, the*
> *glorious Father, may give you the Spirit of wisdom and*
> *revelation, so that you may know Him better. I pray that*
> *the eyes of your heart may be enlightened in order that*
> *you may know the hope to which He has called you, the*
> *riches of His glorious inheritance in His holy people, and*
> *His incomparably great power for us who believe.*

When I reflect on how far things have come in my life, I cannot help but think of what God's Word says in Ecclesiastes 3:11:

> *He has made everything beautiful in its time. He has also*
> *set eternity in the human heart; yet no one can fathom*
> *what God has done from beginning to end.*

Still, the prodigal journey is different for every child. Some kids really take the long, long, winding path. Some take destructive paths. Some unfortunately need to experience the lowest of lows before they return to God.

It is interesting to me that the father in the parable of the prodigal son didn't rush out to look for his son. He didn't search for him or try to rescue him from his circumstances. He didn't send his servants out to go and find him or force him to come back home. In fact, he did nothing. It seems he simply went about his own business and he waited. I am sure not a day went by that he didn't think of his son, that he didn't wonder what his son was doing or how he was going. There must have been a longing in his heart that never left, and we know for sure that he was always ready to receive his son back. But the father is patient. He waited for his son to come home.

I imagine that the prodigal son wanted to return to his father's house earlier than he did. Perhaps the son thought he had to prove himself worthy first. But at the right time, at his lowest point, he came to the realisation that it would be better to go back to his father. This is often the case with prodigal children—the thing that often compels a prodigal back to God is hitting rock bottom.

It was no different for my son. He had become numb toward the things of God. He had hardened his heart towards God and shut out the Holy Spirit. I watched in dismay as my son turned into someone who had to battle through depression and much emotional turmoil because of his decision to deliberately reject God and His ways, much as I had done at the age of nineteen, towards the end of my own prodigal journey.

We can find hope in the testimonies of many people who have literally been redeemed at the lowest points in their lives. But when it comes to prodigal children, if we chase them, harass them, or try to convince them of their wrongdoing when they are at rock bottom, it's likely that their guilt and shame will only be emphasised, making it harder for them to come back. I don't know of many stories where the strength and striving of parents resulted in the child's return. I think the opposite happens: Through our striving and not letting go we only strain the relationship.

At times I would grow so impatient. It was often hard to stay the course, to believe that my son would return to a relationship with Jesus. I would cry out: "Lord! Why aren't You doing anything?" but not see any changes for the better in his behavior. Thankfully, Jesus is gentle in His approach with us. He doesn't force His way into our lives. He reminded me that He stands and waits, and continually knocks. I would have to learn to wait too.

> *Behold, I stand at the door, and knock. If anyone hears My*
> *voice, and opens the door, I will come in to him and dine*
> *with him, and he with Me.*

> Revelation 3:20 (NKJV)

God is always ready and waiting, and although it causes us angst as parents to see our child stray, we should rest in God's plans for our children. We can hold onto the faith that there will be a good outcome in the end because of Romans 8:28:

> *And we know that in all things God works for the*
> *good of those who love him, who have been called*
> *according to his purpose.*

A HEDGE OF PROTECTION

One day when I was praying for another mother of a prodigal, God showed me the image of a sheep pen. The sheep pen had one entrance, a gate where sheep could freely come in and go out. That was where Jesus was standing as the gatekeeper. There was, however, another opening at the back of the sheep pen, an opening where sheep could be stolen, or be lured away and deceived, or decide to escape and explore on their own, following their own desires.

In this particular image, I saw Jesus enter the back gate where the sheep escape. He was on a war horse that was armoured up for battle. Jesus was dressed in a white robe and as He approached, He simply stated, "She will be found."

This image brought to mind the scripture in James 1:14 where we read that temptation comes from our own desires which entice us and drag us away. There is a back gate that people can find, and if they wander through it, they can lose their way. It also reminded me of the parable of the lost sheep in Matthew 18:10-14, where Jesus is portrayed not as a farmer, but as a shepherd who would do anything to protect His sheep. If even one was lost, He would leave the ninety-nine to search for it. I also thought of David, the Old Testament shepherd-boy who went on to become king. He said to Saul:

> *Your servant used to keep his father's sheep, and when a lion or a bear came and took a lamb out of the flock, I went out after it and struck it, and delivered the lamb from its mouth; and when it arose against me, I caught it by its beard, and struck and killed it. Your servant has killed both lion and bear.*

> *1 Samuel 17:34-36 (NKJV)*

Shepherds were not faint-hearted or weak! They were fierce protectors who would do everything in their power to rescue the lost sheep.

The other part of the revelation was that Jesus was riding on a war horse—not on a pony, a donkey or a camel, but on an armoured horse as one prepared for battle, a battle He already knew was won. When He said the words, "She will be found," He spoke calmy about the prodigal child we were praying for.

As He spoke those words, the image changed, and I saw another picture, this time of a very large, square hedge maze. It had a distinct boundary, and had only one entry or exit point. The message was clear—even if this prodigal was lost, she would not be able to go very far! I was able to encourage her mother that there were going to be moments when her daughter would get to a particular point and have to stop. Just as in a maze, she would sometimes be able to go no further, where she had no option but to turn around.

The reality is, that however 'wild' our children's behaviour may get, their lives are still under God's control. Jesus is on a mission and when we as parents join Him, we may feel like there is nothing we can do physically, but spiritually He is in perfect control of the situation.

A BANQUETING TABLE

Not only is Jesus fighting for our children, He also provides what *we* need as parents. I saw this one day when God showed me an image of a banquet table. On the large, rectangular table was a white tablecloth and food spread out from one end to the other. Around the table were long wooden benches.

There were absolutely no rules at this table. The King, sitting at the table, was relaxed and welcoming. The benches around the table were full of people. Some had been sitting there a short time; some seemed to have been there for maybe hours or days. As I walked into the room, the King immediately noticed I had entered and waved to me to come closer. He tapped the seat right next to Him and started telling people to move up, to make space next to Him for His child. This was my time! As I took some food in my hands, I knew that I had the ear of the King and that, although He already knew my need, I could tell Him anything.

The food at the table represents all our needs and desires. Everything God, the King, owns is laid out waiting for us to come and receive. Some people aren't sure where to sit—they do not know their rightful place as a child of God. But God delights in seeing us. Our needs are met simply by 'sitting' at the table. There God listens to us. He wants to hear about our burdens, our heart-state. He listens, and He fixes things. The banquet is set up! Everything we need or want is available at the banquet table, but the richest food and most abundant supply of blessing are nearest to God. If we want the best, we have to get closer to Him. Matthew 6:33 (NKJV) says:

> *Seek first the kingdom of God and His righteousness, and*
> *all these things shall be added to you.*

In the time of stress, we may forget to sit at this heavenly table. We tend to rush through our days, but God asks us to sit, even for a few minutes. I urge you—don't push time with Him aside in favour of other things.

As I navigated the prodigal season with my son, understanding the picture of the banquet table helped me to stay close in my relationship with the Lord. It showed me how welcoming He was and how deeply He desired my companionship. That's what He wants for all of us! He wants us to join Him there. The closer we come, the more we feel loved, and the more we bring our prayers and worries to Him, the more He can fix! How wonderful to know that the nearer we are to Him, the more abundant is our King's provision. When we are seated with Him, we know that our future—and that of our prodigal—is secure because we are sons and daughters of the King!

8

WALKING IN CONFIDENCE

A S PARENTS, WE DON'T ALWAYS SEE THINGS clearly. We judge according to what we see with our natural eyes or in the natural world, when in fact, God is a supernatural God. We know His plans are for good—that He has a hope and a future planned for our children from the time they are formed in the womb. But because God is Spirit, we must see with spiritual eyes if we are to partner with Him for our children's destiny.

In 2 Kings 6:15-17 we have an example of a man whose eyes were opened to see a situation as God saw it. We read:

> *When Elisha's servant got up and went out early the*
> *next morning, an army with horses and chariots had*
> *surrounded the city. 'Oh no, my lord! What shall we do?'*
> *the servant asked. 'Don't be afraid,' Elisha answered.*
> *'Those who are with us are more than those who are with*
> *them.' And Elisha prayed, 'Open his eyes, LORD, so that he*
> *may see.' Then the LORD opened the servant's eyes, and he*

*looked and saw the hills full of horses and chariots of fire
all around Elisha.*

Imagine an army, a spiritual army that fights on our behalf! God is active in the unseen realms. Oh what joy they must have felt when He revealed this to Elisha and to Elisha's servant! I can only imagine how the servant's hope increased at the sight of the spiritual army God had provided to help them fight the enemy.

If you are in the midst of a battle for your child, my heartfelt advice is: Pray to God! As you align your prayers with His heart, God will show you a picture or share a verse with you. This will increase your faith and enable you to hold fast to God throughout your child's prodigal journey. It increases our faith because faith is "the substance of things hoped for" (Hebrews 11:1 NKJV). When we see how God will fulfil His promises, we are filled with hope. Faith arises when we pray into that which God has already seen and made known to us. In praying for Daniel, I turned Jeremiah 29:11 into a declaration:

"Lord, I thank You that the plans You have for my son are to prosper him and not to harm him. God, You formed him in the womb and You know exactly how and when he will turn back to You. Whatever he needs to turn his heart towards You, do it, Lord!"

So rest in God! You can be sure that when the victory comes and the prodigal returns, there will be a celebration. But realise ultimately that this is a supernatural work, not one done in the flesh, and when the victory is won, all the glory belongs to God.

TURNING VISION INTO PRAYER

Whenever I get an image from God, I seek a verse or portion of Scripture that aligns with what God has revealed to me. I want to know that what I have seen and the prayers I will pray are backed up with

Scripture. This spares me from clinging to false hope or praying only from my own will. Instead, I can be assertive as I pray, convinced that as I pray, I am effectively wielding the living, active Word of God like a two-edged sword! This is why I encourage you to write down every positive, life-filled word whispered to your heart. After all, how will we remember His words if we don't have a record? Hold fast to every tiny seed given to you. Let it soak in, let it become your mustard seed of faith!

Matthew 17:14-20 recounts a time when the disciples tried to cast a demon out of a boy. In that account, we read that Jesus told the disciples that the reason they failed to cast the demon out was because they had so little faith. Then He goes on to say, "Truly I tell you, if you have faith as small as a mustard seed, you can say to this mountain, 'Move from here to there,' and it will move. Nothing will be impossible for you."

Take a moment to reflect on those 'seeds of faith' God has given you. Perhaps you already have a verse or picture for your child. If not, take time to seek the Lord, and remember it may come when you least expect it. It may come in the form of a word from someone else or an encouragement or verse from a pastor or friend. Maybe someone has already told you something about your child and you discounted it. Ask God to help your unbelief!

Mark's Gospel also tells the story of the boy who needed to be set free of a demon spirit. As in Matthew's account, the disciples were unable to cast the demon out. I'm sure this may have caused them frustration and I wonder about the doubt that must have been cast over them. But Mark's Gospel focusses on the father of the boy. When Jesus arrives on the scene, He engages in a discussion with the father. "Everything is possible for one who believes," says Jesus. In reply, the father exclaims, "I do believe; help me overcome my unbelief!" (Mark 9:24).

May this story speak to you today. You may have already come in faith and been disappointed. It's okay. Ask again. Let the Lord reveal things to you in His time. It wasn't until later in the story, when the disciples asked Jesus why they could not cast the demon out, that Jesus explained that this kind of demon could only be driven out by prayer.

The truth is, God doesn't want you to suffer through this journey. I can attest to the faithfulness of God through my son's prodigal time, that God is gracious and His mercies are endless. One of these mercies was that while we were battling for our son's salvation, our other sons were doing well. God sustained and took care of my other two boys and their faith journeys while we battled it out for the one who needed assistance. It was like a saucepan boiling over on the stove because the temperature is set too high—I was thankful that as one was on high, two other pots were just simmering! It was what we could handle at the time.

We have a loving Father, a God who created and loves your child more than you do. He does not want to keep secrets from us. He comes to relieve our stresses, to release us from worry. He gives us hope by revealing to us the plans He has for our prodigal child.

* * *

Is another person's salvation worth praying for? When I see what my son went through in his time of wandering away from God, I have to say "yes." I am more convinced than ever of the earthly rewards *and* the eternal rewards that are at stake. Jesus has saved my son's life! I've witnessed his transformation from being constantly glum and depressed to walking out the abundant life Jesus offers.

Since then, my husband and I have picked up the baton of prayer that was dropped in our parents' generation. We know it is worth contending for our children and spending ourselves in prayer to see a loved one come to the Lord. As 1 Peter 1:6-7 says:

> *In all this you greatly rejoice, though now for a little*
> *while you may have had to suffer grief in all kinds of*

*trials. These have come so that the proven genuineness of
your faith—of greater worth than gold, which perishes
even though refined by fire—may result in praise, glory
and honour when Jesus Christ is revealed.*

There is so much more to our children's salvation than simply receiving Jesus. While a prodigal lives in survival mode, when they return home to the Father they have a future to look forward to. I love watching our children grow both physically and spiritually. In every stage of our children's lives, we are able to witness the maturity and growth they have gone through and come to. 1 John 2:12-14 puts it like this:

*I am writing to you, dear children, because your sins have
been forgiven on account of his name... (and) because
you know the Father... I write to you, fathers, because
you know him who is from the beginning... I write to you,
young men, because you are strong, and the word of God
lives in you, and you have overcome the evil one.*

How wonderful that we can enjoy growing up in the Lord's ways, that we can begin knowing our sins are forgiven and go on to know the Father! I love this concept of progress in our relationship with the Father, Son, and Holy Spirit—that there is always something more for us to grow into. Parenting a prodigal is a mission, but there is something God desires to develop in you. You will gain a prize—not just the salvation of your child, but the greater prize of what God is doing in your own life.

Before my son turned away, I had trouble understanding what it was like for parents of prodigals. Now I have much more compassion for what these parents go through. I also have increased faith in this area and have a passionate desire to see prodigals return to personal relationship with Christ and with God the Father. My prayer is that my testimony will be a source of renewed hope for others who are parenting prodigals. I pray you will not fall into the trap of being jealous of other families who seem to have an easier road, but that you will know the real gift of the situation—the opportunity to grow closer to God and closer to your son or daughter. May you experience fresh power in prayer as you hear from God. God wants to talk to you! He wants to reveal bigger plans, so that we are not stuck in the current problem but can look to the future and believe according to what He shows us. I pray that you, just like me, will experience a season of spiritual growth as you wait for your child to come home to God.

As I reflect on my life prior to going through the journey of having a prodigal, I realise that although I was comfortable in my relationship with God, I was not spiritually confident. Now, I am. I took much for granted, and when my son walked away from the church and from God, it challenged my own faith. But it was in that challenge that God proved Himself faithful in all things. I had always expected that just because I was a faithful Christian, my son would follow. But God wants each of us to come to their own realisation of their need for Him. I can now truly say that although I have been through an extremely difficult season, I am glad to have walked through it, and I can now even say that I am blessed to have had a prodigal child!

EPILOGUE

IT'S BEEN THREE YEARS SINCE OUR SON began his journey of faith with Jesus. Since then, all three boys have been on their own spiritual journey.

It reminds me of a picture I saw of an orchard with many fruit trees. There were orange trees full of fruit, and I understood that these were *my* trees in the orchard. Then I saw other trees with a different kind of fruit; these were my husband's fruit trees. I found it interesting that although we were married, we did not have a mixed-fruit orchard, with orange-lime trees, or orange-pear trees. Each person's fruit trees in the orchard were specific to them. I expected to see that the trees in our children's orchards would be a combination of my husband's and mine, but this was not the case either. One had cherry trees and another had banana trees, and although they were growing close to each other, they were separate orchards. Some didn't seem to take up much space but their trees contained a lot of fruit.

I marvelled at this picture and realised that this is why we have to fight for our children's salvation—because our children's lives need to bear fruit! The fruit they produce will be as unique as they are, and they have a responsibility to grow an orchard of their own, to bear the fruit they were created for. Thankfully, God knows the exact conditions they need, and He prepares the soil that will ensure a harvest of fruit.

Just as each of our children's fruit is unique, so, too, are their journeys. Funnily enough, the tables have turned and it is Daniel who is concerned about his brothers now that they are at the same age he was when he wandered away. He doesn't want them to make the same mistakes that he did! But I have seen the work of the Lord in the lives of my children and I am filled with confidence and expectation for their futures. My middle son hasn't rebelled or had as wild a journey as Daniel's, but he is still on an adventure of his own to discover the truth that sets us free. Our youngest only became a teenager in the past year, so it's early days to see what his journey will look like and whether he too will rebel for a time. But I can say this: I am not afraid. Rebellion, insecurity, the search for independence, love and truth is a natural part of every teenager or young adult's journey, and in their quest for answers, some will take paths we would rather they didn't. If that happens, we must remember that no amount of worldly wisdom or knowledge can bring a prodigal home; only God can do that. He has set eternity in every heart (Ecclesiastes 3:11) and He is faithful to call them home. Surrender your child—and yourself—to Him. Then watch for the miracles He will do!

JOURNALLING GUIDE

1. *As a parent of a prodigal, what are your greatest fears?*

_____

_____

_____

_____

_____

_____

_____

_____

_____

_____

2. *What does God say in response to those fears?*

_____

_____

_____

_____

_____

_____

_____

_____

_____

_____

3. *What do you know to be true, not necessarily because you can see it in the physical realm, but because it is true from God's perspective?*

_____

_____

_____

_____

_____

_____

_____

_____

4. *Who is journeying with you through this season? Who could you invite to walk with you through this season?*

_____

_____

_____

_____

_____

_____

_____

_____

_____

5. *Is a friend or youth pastor reaching out to your child? How could you show your appreciation, or encourage them?*

_____

_____

_____

_____

_____

_____

_____

_____

_____

6. *Do you know the calling or anointing on your child's life? How might you remind your child of their God-given destiny and worth, regardless of their choices or behaviour?*

_____

_____

_____

_____

_____

_____

_____

_____

_____

7. *Does your child show signs of being depressed? If so, what professional help could you seek out? If not, what are the indicators that encourage you that your child is doing okay despite wandering from the faith?*

_____

_____

_____

_____

_____

_____

_____

_____

8. *Is there a specific word, promise, verse or perspective that God has revealed to you about your situation? How could you use that revelation to contend for breakthrough in your son or daughter's life?*

_____

_____

_____

_____

_____

_____

_____

_____

_____

9. *Try writing out your own prayer for your child. On days when you don't know how to pray, this can be a good place to start!*

_____

_____

_____

_____

_____

_____

_____

_____

10. *Reflect on what you are personally learning right now. Are there questions you would like to ask God? What areas are being challenged in your own life? What spiritual gifts are being stirred in you through this experience? What advice would you give to others who are walking a similar road?*

_____

_____

_____

_____

_____

_____

_____

_____

PRAYERS FOR A
PRODIGAL

Prayers For A Prodigal

Father, Thank You that my _____ will be found by You, that (he/she) is so important to You. Thank You that You leave the ninety-nine to search for the one that is lost. Thank You, Lord Jesus, that You are the Good Shepherd, that You know where (he/she) is, and that you will rescue (him/her). We pray that _____ would experience frustration as (he/she) tries to do things that are against Your will, God, and that You would place a hedge of protection around (him/her).

Thank You, God, that You created _____. I declare that (He/She) is Your workmanship, and that You knew (him/her) even before You formed (him/her) in the womb. Lord, we thank You that You know _____ now. Lord, watch over _____ , protect (him/her). Lord, You know what it is to be tempted. I pray You would help my child to resist temptation and overcome sin. I pray, Lord, that the enemy would not be able to lie to (him/her) anymore. Lord, your will is that all should come to know Christ, and I pray that the day of salvation for _____ will be today.

Oh God, thank You that you hear the prayers of the righteous. Please forgive me of anything I have done to contribute to _____ 's prodigal journey. Lord, please show me what I need to pray about right now in my child's journey. I thank You, Jesus, that You intercede for my child, and I ask You to show me how to align my prayers with Yours at this time.

Lord, You are close to the broken-hearted, You are aware of my heart's cry. You see my tears, You hear my cries, and I trust You to answer.

Lord, I pray Your protection over _____. I pray that no weapon formed against (him/her) will stand, that You, Lord, will bring emotional, mental and physical healing to my _____. Lord, I pray that the veil on (his/her) eyes would come off and that Your name will be glorified. You have the victory over sin and death. Lord God, I pray that Your Holy Spirit will draw _____ to Yourself, that (he/she) will follow when You call (his/her) name.

Lord God, I pray that You would open _____'s eyes to see Your works. Let them remember Your goodness and return to You. Oh Lord, I ask that You would heal every hurt, every offence they have experienced. I pray that the root of bitterness that has taken hold would be broken, that they will confess their sin and return to You to be made whole. May not one of Your words return to You void. May _____ remember the God of (his/her) youth. I pray against the lies of the enemy that would keep my _____ bound or feeling guilty and ashamed. I pray that You would intervene today. _____'s life depends on You, and I pray protection over (him/her) right now. I pray (he/she) would meet other Christians, and that (he/she) may experience Your goodness and mercy.

Oh God, I'm weary, overcome with worry for my child. Lord, You have seen every tear. I pray that You will call my _____ by name and that (he/she) will be saved. Lord, You are not far from me, and You care for me. I thank You that the prayer of the righteous avails much!

Lord, deliver _____ from evil. I pray that (his/her) heart may be made soft. Soften (his/her) heart, Lord, to Your voice. Let (him/her) hear Your voice, Lord! You know the plans you have for _____. They are good plans, plans not to harm (him/her) but to give (him/her) a hope and a future. I pray that You would protect my _____. Let (him/her) become a child of God. I pray that You will call (him/her) clearly and lovingly today.

Lord Jesus, You are the Way, the Truth and the Life. Father, I pray that _____ will discern between lies and truth, that (he/she) will desire the abundant life that can only come by knowing and surrendering to You, Lord Jesus. Thank You that You are the Shepherd of the lost sheep. Help _____ to find (his/her) way back to You. Holy Spirit, thank You for actively working to bring _____ back to the Father. I bring my child to You today in Jesus' name. Amen

ACKNOWLEDGEMENTS

I don't take writing a book for granted. Although this book is a fulfilment of a prophecy, writing from the heart and personal experience can be a demanding process. I thank God for giving me wisdom and for His grace to write this book.

My biggest thanks go to the most important people in my life:

To my husband, Marco. Thank you for your steadfastness and staying the course with me during this trial in our lives. You helped me keep looking forward, and we are better and stronger for it. I appreciate your tenacity as we reach for greater goals!

To my sons. Thank you for the daily gifts and growth you bring to our lives. We are thankful for you, we love you, and we enjoy parenting you. Daniel, you are a testimony of the love and faithfulness of God. Thank you for allowing me to share part of your story. May God use this story for His continued glory.

To my parents. Parenting is ever evolving, and knowing what to do and when is an art, as I'm finding out. Thank you for your unfailing love and support over the years.

To my church family. Thank you for being spiritual fathers and mothers, brothers and sisters who walk by faith. You may not see the full extent of your impact here on earth but know that I thank God for you in my life.

Thanks also to those who worked on this book at its different stages:

To Gwen Parkhill. Thank you for reading this book in its initial drafts. You were brave, and it is a pleasure to know you. Thank you for your probing questions that helped me to put the 'meat on the bones' to bring this story to life.

To Anya McKee at Torn Curtain Publishing. Thank you for taking on the publishing of this book. Once again you and your team have polished up a rough diamond and have made it possible for this book to get into the hands of grateful parents.

We hope you enjoyed this book!

For more inspiring content from Eleanor Formaggio,
including videos, resources and tools for spiritual growth,
visit www.heldcontent.com *or join our online community*
on Facebook or Instagram @Eleanorformaggio.

To enquire about events and speaking, contact:
info@heldcontent.com

CPSIA information can be obtained
at www.ICGtesting.com
Printed in the USA
LVHW061228280323
PP17700000001B/3

9 780645 397710